Applying the Standards:
Evidence-Based Reading
Grade 3

Credits
Content Editor: Elise Craver
Copy Editor: Angela Triplett

Visit *carsondellosa.com* for correlations to Common Core, state, national, and Canadian provincial standards.

Carson-Dellosa Publishing LLC
PO Box 35665
Greensboro, NC 27425 USA
carsondellosa.com

ISBN 978-1-4838-1461-2
04-002181151

Table of Contents

Introduction

The purpose of this book is to engage students in close reading while applying the standards. The Common Core reading and language strands are reflected in the interactive questions that follow each passage.

The lessons are intended to help students not only comprehend what they read superficially, but also to help them read complex texts closely and analytically. Students need to get involved deeply with what they are reading and use higher-order thinking skills to reflect on what they have read.

On the following activity pages, students will read a variety of literature and informational passages. These are brief but lend themselves to more complex thinking. Given the opportunity to study shorter texts, students can better practice the higher-level skills they need to closely read more demanding texts.

Each selection is followed by text-dependent questions. Students are prompted to pay attention to how a text is organized, to solve the question of why the author chose specific words, to look for deeper meaning, and to determine what the author is trying to say.

Use the included rubric to guide assessment of student responses and further plan any necessary remediation. The art of close reading is an invaluable skill that will help students succeed in their school years and beyond.

Common Core Alignment Chart

Use this chart to plan your instruction, practice, or remediation of a specific standard. To do this, first choose your targeted standard; then, find the pages listed on the chart that correlate to the standard.

Common Core State Standards*		Practice Pages
Reading Standards for Literature		
Key Ideas and Details	3.RL.1–3.RL.3	5–7, 9, 11, 13, 15, 16, 18, 19, 21–25, 27
Craft and Structure	3.RL.4–3.RL.6	5, 6, 9, 11, 13, 15, 16, 19, 21–25, 27
Integration of Knowledge and Ideas	3.RL.7, 3.RL.9	24, 27
Range of Reading and Level of Text Complexity	3.RL.10	Each reading passage can be adapted to exercise this standard.
Reading Standards for Informational Text		
Key Ideas and Details	3.RI.1–3.RI.3	28–32, 34, 35, 37–42, 44, 46–48, 50, 51, 53, 54, 56, 57, 59, 61, 62
Craft and Structure	3.RI.4–3.RI.6	29–31, 34, 35, 37–40, 44, 46–48, 50, 53, 56, 57, 61, 62
Integration of Knowledge and Ideas	3.RI.7–3.RI.9	28–30, 32, 34, 35, 37, 38, 40–42, 44, 46, 48, 50, 51, 53, 54, 56, 57, 59, 61, 62
Range of Reading and Level of Text Complexity	3.RI.10	Each reading passage can be adapted to exercise this standard.
Reading Standards: Foundational Skills		
Fluency	3.RF.4	Each reading passage can be adapted to exercise this standard.
Language Standards		
Conventions of Standard English	3.L.1–3.L.2	30
Knowledge of Language	3.L.3	6, 16, 22, 27, 39, 61
Vocabulary Acquisition and Use	3.L.4–3.L.6	9, 13, 21–25, 27, 29, 30, 34, 35, 38, 41, 46, 47, 50, 53, 54, 61

Reading Comprehension Rubric

Use this rubric as a guide to assess students' written work. It can also be offered to students to help them check their work or as a tool to show your scoring.

4	_____ Offers insightful reasoning and strong evidence of critical thinking _____ Makes valid, nontrivial inferences based on evidence in the text _____ Skillfully supports answers with relevant details from the text _____ Gives answers that indicate a complete understanding of the text _____ Gives answers that are easy to understand, clear, and concise _____ Uses conventions, spelling, and grammar correctly
3	_____ Offers sufficient reasoning and evidence of critical thinking _____ Makes inferences based on evidence in the text _____ Supports answers with details from the text _____ Gives answers that indicate a good understanding of the text _____ Gives answers that are easy to understand _____ Uses conventions, spelling, and grammar correctly most of the time
2	_____ Demonstrates some evidence of critical thinking _____ Makes incorrect inferences or does not base inferences on evidence in the text _____ Attempts to support answers with information from the text _____ Gives answers that indicate an incomplete understanding of the text _____ Gives answers that are understandable but lack focus _____ Gives answers containing several errors in conventions, spelling, and grammar
1	_____ Demonstrates limited or no evidence of critical thinking _____ Makes no inferences _____ Does not support answers with details from the text _____ Gives answers that indicate little to no understanding of the text _____ Gives answers that are difficult to understand _____ Gives answers with many errors in conventions, spelling, and grammar

Name _____

Read. Then, answer the questions.

The Science Project

Ms. Hagen had insisted that every student enter the science fair this year. Kyle was assigned Seth as a partner, much to Kyle's disappointment. Everyone knew that Seth was the laziest kid in the class. He never finished his assignments, and he was always doodling rather than listening. The boys decided to meet at Kyle's house after school to plan their project.

Seth arrived with a backpack bursting with test tubes, magnets, and crystals. Kyle was surprised. Why would this lazy kid have such cool stuff? When Kyle suggested building a model of the solar system, Seth pulled out painted foam balls and rattled off all types of facts about each model planet. Maybe Kyle had been mistaken about Seth.

At last, the boys agreed to experiment to find the best place to store bananas. The boys met each day after school and were confident that their project would be the best. Kyle worked on writing the report, while Seth continued to question and experiment further. They found they made quite a team.

Ms. Hagen told Kyle that she was proud of him for helping Seth with the project. Kyle had to explain that Seth was responsible for much of the work. He went on to ask if Seth could be his partner for next month's math project.

1. Why was Kyle disappointed to have Seth assigned as his partner for the project?

_____

_____

2. The author describes Kyle as being *surprised*. What was Kyle surprised about?

_____

_____

3. How did Kyle's thinking change through the story? Use evidence from the text to support your answer.

_____

_____

_____

☀ Reflect

The author ends by hinting that Kyle and Seth may work together on a future project. Why? Describe how the story would be different if the last sentence were not included.

_____

_____

Name _____

Read. Then, answer the questions.

The Bremen-Town Musicians

A long time ago, there lived an old donkey who had faithfully served his master for many years. The donkey had since become too old to carry sacks of grain, and his master planned to do away with him. The donkey developed a plan to run away to the town of Bremen where he would become a musician. The donkey had not gone too far when he came upon an old hunting dog lying in the road. The dog explained that he had become too old to hunt any longer, and that his master had plans to do away with him.

The donkey suggested that the dog join him in Bremen to become a musician. The dog agreed, and the two of them continued their journey. Farther down the road, the friends happened upon an old cat and an old rooster, both fearing for their lives as well. They decided to join the donkey and the dog. As night fell, the four travelers became tired and hungry. They spotted a house in the woods and approached it. Peering in, they found a table full of food and a band of robbers sitting around it. The four friends screeched out their music as loud as they could, scaring the robbers away.

After the animals had eaten their fill and fallen asleep, the robbers came back to the house. They saw the cat's eyes reflecting light and began to run. The dog bit their legs, the donkey kicked them, and the rooster crowed. The robbers were so scared they never returned to the house again.

1. Why did the donkey decide to run away and become a musician?

_____

2. What trait do all of the animals that journey to Bremen share?

_____

3. Why did the author use the word *screeched* to describe how the animals performed their music?

_____

_____

4. How did the animals' unique style of music help them solve a problem?

_____

_____

✺ Reflect

Would the conflict have been solved the same way if the animals had been able to make traditional music? Why or why not? Use evidence from the text to support your answer.

_____

_____

Read. Then, answer the questions.

The Vanishing School Supplies

"Mom, I need more pencils for school tomorrow. I think I should get a lot," Timothy said as he jumped in the car.

"Wow, you must really be working hard. You have used so many school supplies already. Last week you needed scissors, and the week before that it was markers," replied Timothy's mother.

The next morning, Timothy put two packs of brand new pencils in his backpack. When his mother picked him up, Timothy said, "Hey, Mom, can we swing by the store to get more colored pencils?"

"What?" Timothy's mother asked. "Timothy Avery, what is going on? You cannot possibly be using all of your supplies this quickly."

"Well, I am sharing them. It all started when Gerardo made fun of Pete's pencil. It was almost completely used up and the eraser was totally gone. It looked pretty bad. Then, Pete said that his family could not buy any more pencils until his dad got paid again. So I started thinking about it and realized that Pete never had his own scissors or markers, so I gave him mine."

"Timothy, I am very proud of you. I have an idea. Let's invite Pete to get ice cream with us after school tomorrow. I think the two of you could learn a lot from each other."

1. At first, why does Timothy's mom think he needs so many supplies?

_____

2. How does Timothy's mom react when he asks for more colored pencils?

_____

_____

3. At the end of the story, why is Timothy's mother proud of him?

_____

_____

Reflect

Based on the story, what types of things do you think Timothy and Pete can learn from each other?

_____

_____

_____

Name _____

Read. Then, answer the questions on page 9.

Grandpa Remembers

My grandpa lived just down the lane and around the corner from my family. I loved to go to his house and spend time with him. He taught me how to fish and play checkers. In the wintertime, we would sit by the fire and play games. In the summertime, we would go for long walks. **Time flew** with my grandpa. My favorite times with Grandpa were the "remembering" times. Grandpa loved to tell stories about how things used to be. Grandpa always said he hoped he didn't **talk my ear off**. But, I loved to listen to Grandpa's stories.

"One cold winter's day when I wasn't much older than you," Grandpa began, "I begged to go with my dad to harvest a crop of ice blocks."

"A crop of ice blocks? You're **pulling my leg**, Grandpa," I interrupted.

"I am not pulling your leg," stated Grandpa. "Where was I? Oh yes. When I was young, people didn't have refrigerators like they do now. Gathering ice blocks was the only way to keep foods cold through the spring and summer," Grandpa explained.

"I helped my dad get the tractor and wagon hooked up. Then, we drove down to the river. When we got there, Dad tested the ice. 'Looks like we found an excellent stretch of ice,' he said. Then, he took out the logging saw. A logging saw is a long saw with handles at each end. I watched as my dad put the saw in the water. Pushing and then pulling, he cut a long slab of ice. Then, I helped him move the slab up the bank to the wagon. He let me hold onto one end of the saw, and we worked together to cut the slab into square blocks. Then, my dad used large ice tongs to put the blocks of ice on the wagon. When the ice blocks were loaded, we **hit the road** and headed to the ice shed. The ice shed had three or four inches of sawdust on the floor. We put the blocks on top of the sawdust. Then, we packed more sawdust around the blocks. We stored all of our food that needed to stay cold inside the ice shed."

The remembering times were some of my favorite times with my grandpa. It was fun to **shoot the breeze** with him and learn about how things were when he was my age. I will always remember our remembering times. Someday, I would like to have remembering times with my grandchildren.

Read the story on page 8. Then, answer the questions.

1. Choose one of the bold phrases, such as *time flew* or *hit the road*. Explain what the phrase means.

_____

_____

2. What activities do Grandpa and the narrator do together?

_____

_____

3. What are "remembering" times? Explain how you know.

_____

_____

_____

_____

4. How are "remembering" times related to the central message of the story?

_____

_____

_____

Reflect

Read the last sentence of the story. Why do you think the narrator ends the story this way?

_____

_____

_____

_____

_____

_____

_____

_____

Read. Then, answer the questions on page 11.

Left Alone

Derrick shouted good-bye and waved to his friends as he ran up the front walk. He had come straight home from school today. He was eager to play his new computer game. Derrick turned the knob of the front door. It was locked!

Derrick's mom was always home from work before he got home. She worked at a bookstore and left each day at three o'clock. It was 3:45, and she still wasn't home.

Derrick was worried about his mom, but he decided to try to get into the house. He walked around the house and tried the side door. It was locked. The back door was locked, too. He thought a few minutes about climbing in through a window. Derrick thought his mom might be angry if he bent a screen or broke something while trying to climb in the window.

Derrick felt his throat tighten and tears come to his eyes. He decided he wouldn't cry, and he wiped his eyes. "Think," he said to himself.

Just then, Derrick's neighbor drove up her driveway. He was so relieved. He ran right over to her. "My mom isn't home, and I can't get in the house!" he shouted in one breath.

His neighbor said, "Come on in, Derrick. You can call your mom and wait here for her." Derrick followed Mrs. Park into the house. He sat at the kitchen counter. Mrs. Park gave him two cookies and a glass of water.

Derrick called the bookstore where his mom worked. Her boss said that she had left work on time. As Derrick hung up the phone, he felt his stomach tighten again. He wondered what could have happened to her. Derrick started to dial his grandma's phone number. At that moment, he saw his mom's car pull up in the driveway. He thanked Mrs. Park and raced out the door.

Derrick ran straight to his mom. She stepped out of the car and into his hug. "I'm so sorry," she said. "I was stuck in traffic on the highway. There was a terrible accident. My car didn't move for 20 minutes. All I could think about was you waiting for me. Are you okay?"

Derrick told his mother what he had done. And, he said, "I wasn't worried for a minute."

Name _____

Read the story on page 10. Then, answer the questions.

1. What details made Derrick start to worry about his mom?

_____

_____

2. How does the author show that Derrick was feeling upset about his mom not being home?

_____

_____

3. Later in the story, what makes Derrick worry even more?

_____

_____

4. How was Derrick's mom feeling while she was stuck in traffic? How do you know?

_____

_____

_____

☀ Reflect

At the end of the story, why do you think Derrick tells his mom that he "wasn't worrried"? Use evidence from the story to support your answer.

_____

_____

_____

_____

_____

_____

_____

_____

Name _____

Read. Then, answer the questions on page 13.

The Family Hike

We started on the trail early in the morning. The sun was rising in the sky, and the air around us was cold and misty. The pine trees looked like arrows pointing our way to the top of the mountain. It was a wonderful morning.

My mom and dad each carried a heavy backpack full of food, tents, water, and other things. Ben and I carried packs too. Mine only had my clothes and sleeping bag in it. I carried a few snacks in my pockets and two water bottles on my belt. Ben is bigger than I am, so he also carried some food and a cookstove in his pack.

We walked quietly at first. My dad says you don't need words to be part of the forest in the morning. I could hear birds singing and chipmunks moving through the leaves on the ground. There was no breeze, so the trees were silent. We walked single file along the trail.

At lunchtime, we stopped by a stream that flowed down the mountain. We could see a small waterfall higher up, but here the water cut through the rock and snaked past flowers and bushes. We took off our shoes and dipped our feet in the water. The sun shone brightly overhead, and we all took off our jackets.

I knew better than to ask how much farther we had to go. My parents always say that our destination is the hike itself. We would be walking for three days on these trails. We would see many beautiful sights and hear and smell things we don't hear or smell at home in the city. My mom and dad are teachers. Every summer, we take a trip as a family. Ben wanted to bring a teenage friend, but my dad said that this was family time. Ben complained, but I know he likes family trips too.

At dinnertime, we stopped and set up our tents on a flat meadow. We could see the next mountain peak from our site. It looked beautiful as the sun set behind it. We built a fire and cooked dinner. We stayed awake a little while longer to watch the stars. My mom pointed out several constellations. I want to be an astronomer someday.

We went to bed soon after dinner because we were all tired from walking. Tomorrow, we will have another long walk. We will reach the top of the mountain before dark. I have never stood on a mountaintop before. My dad says that I will be able to see forever. I think I'll like that. Maybe I will be able to see my friend Ginny's house back home. I will wave to her and shout hello. I'll hear the echo and pretend that she shouted back at me. But, that is tomorrow, and my dad says that even the night is part of the journey. So, I will close my eyes and listen for the owls, the wind in the trees, and the sound of my dad snoring. I love this place!

Name _____

Read the story on page 12. Then, answer the questions.

1. In the first paragraph, what does it mean when the narrator describes the pine trees as looking "like arrows"?

_____

_____

2. How does the narrator feel about the family hike?

_____

_____

3. What details in the story support your answer to question 2?

_____

_____

_____

4. Compare and contrast how the narrator, Ben, and the narrator's parents feel about the hiking trip. Use evidence from the story to support your answer.

_____

_____

_____

_____

☀ Reflect

The narrator's parents say things like "you don't need words to be part of the forest," "our destination is the hike itself," and "even the night is part of the journey." How do these phrases explain how they feel about the hike?

_____

_____

_____

_____

_____

_____

Name _____

Read. Then, answer the questions on page 15.

Sailing in a Storm

Tia and her dad loved to go sailing together. One summer, they decided to sail to High Island. They put the boat in the water in Charlevoix, Michigan, around six o'clock on a Thursday night. They planned to dock the boat, shop and eat in town, and then set out for the island in the morning. Unfortunately, the marina didn't have any available docks for their boat. They had no other choice but cross the lake to the island that night.

Mr. Peters and Tia motored the 23-foot sailboat through the channel and out onto Lake Michigan. It was a quiet evening. The sky was clear, and there was no wind. Mr. Peters put up the sails, but they just flopped lightly in the calm air. The motor pushed them across the wide water. They listened to music and ate cheese and avocado sandwiches.

Around ten o'clock, a brisk wind picked up suddenly. They turned off the motor and sailed with the wind. Very quickly, the wind grew too strong and the waves became large. The small boat leaned over and raced through the water as the wind filled the sails.

When water started splashing into the boat, Mr. Peters shouted, "We have to take down the sails! I can't handle this much wind!" Tia was scared. Her dad wanted her to go up on deck and take down the sails. She was afraid that a wave might wash her overboard or that she might lose her balance. She decided to stay back and steer the boat instead. But, Tia didn't like that either. It was hard to control the boat in the strong wind.

Mr. Peters went up on deck to take down the sails. Tia was shivering. The cold water was soaking her each time the boat crashed through a wave. But, she was shaking more from fear than cold. What would she do if her dad fell into the water? She didn't think she could turn the boat around to get him. She wondered if they would ever make it to the island.

Once Mr. Peters had tied up the sails, he took over the steering. Soon, the waves grew smaller, the wind died down, and several stars appeared in the sky as the clouds moved away. They motored ahead in silence.

When the island came into sight, Tia sat on the bow of the boat and watched. She thought nothing had ever looked so beautiful as the island with its sheltered bay. They anchored the boat in the bay and put up a mooring light. They unrolled their sleeping bags inside the cabin and fell quickly to sleep.

Name _____

Read the story on page 14. Then, answer the questions.

1. What causes Tia and her father to sail to the island that night instead of the next day?

_____

2. How does the author show the reader that Tia is feeling afraid?

_____

_____

_____

3. After the storm dies down, how do Tia and her father react? Compare and contrast their actions before the storm with their actions after the storm.

_____

_____

_____

_____

Reflect

Why does Tia say "nothing had ever looked so beautiful" when she sees the island and its bay? Use details and evidence from the text to support your answer.

_____

_____

_____

_____

_____

_____

_____

_____

_____

_____

_____

Read. Then, answer the questions.

The Small Man

Once upon a time, there was a small man who wanted to be as large as a horse. He asked the horse how he could become the horse's size. The horse told the small man to eat many grains and run around a lot. Immediately, the man did as the horse suggested, but he did not grow.

Next, the small man went to the wise owl. He remembered how the owl had helped solve previous problems. "How can I be as big as my friend the horse?" he asked.

"Why do you want to be bigger than you are?" asked the owl.

"Because if I was bigger, I could win fights," the man replied right away.

"Have you ever needed or wanted to fight before?" the wise owl asked.

The man thought for a moment and soon found his answer. "Why no, I have not ever been in a fight. In fact, I do not even like fighting," the small man answered.

The wise owl smiled, "You see, you are wishing for something that you do not need," he answered. He watched as the small man walked away. He knew the man would **eventually** understand.

1. Why did the man want to be as big as a horse? Underline where you found your answer in the story.

_____

2. How does the owl change the man's thinking?

_____

_____

3. What is the main idea of the story? Explain how you know.

_____

_____

_____

Reflect

Did the owl solve the man's problem? The author uses the word *eventually* in the final sentence of the story. How does that word choice affect your understanding of the story?

_____

_____

_____

Name _____

Read. Then, answer the questions on page 18.

The Bluebird and the Coyote

At one time, Bluebird was not the beautiful blue that she is today. Bluebird did not want to feel plain anymore. Near Bluebird's home was a bright blue lake. No river ran into or out of the lake, so the lake stayed bright blue. Bluebird wished that she was the beautiful blue color of the lake.

Bluebird swam in the lake four times every day for four days. At the end of each day, Bluebird sang this song:

There's a blue water; it lies there.
I went in.
I am all blue.

After Bluebird's fourth swim on the fourth day, she lost all of her feathers. Bluebird was no longer plain, but she was not blue either. After Bluebird swam four times on the fifth day, she grew feathers that were the color of the bright blue lake.

Coyote had been watching Bluebird swim every day for five days. He wanted to jump into the lake with Bluebird, but Coyote was afraid of the water. On the fifth day, after Bluebird grew bright blue feathers, Coyote said to Bluebird, "Why are you no longer plain? Why are you blue and beautiful now? You're more beautiful than any other bird. I want to be blue and beautiful too!"

At that time, Coyote was bright green. Bluebird said to Coyote, "I swam in the lake four times a day for five days. On the fifth day, I became beautiful like the lake." Bluebird even taught Coyote the song that she sang each night.

Coyote did what Bluebird told him. He swam in the lake four times a day for five days. He even sang Bluebird's song at the end of each day. On the fifth day, Coyote was bright blue, just like Bluebird. He was very proud of the way he looked.

Coyote watched in every direction as he walked. He wanted to make sure that everyone saw how beautiful and blue he was. Coyote even looked to see if his shadow had turned blue. He was not watching where he was walking, and he walked right into a tree stump!

Coyote fell down on the road, and he became dirty with dust all over his coat. Coyote was no longer the beautiful, bright blue that he had been. That is why all coyotes today are the color of dirt.

Name _____

Read the story on page 17. Then, answer the questions.

1. What did Bluebird wish for? How did she make her wish come true?

_____

_____

_____

2. What did Coyote fear?

_____

3. Why did Coyote overcome his fear?

_____

_____

4. What character trait caused Coyote to lose the beautiful blue color he had worked so hard for? How?

_____

_____

_____

☀ Reflect

Think about how Coyote's appearance changed over the course of the story. Describe how Coyote's change supports the central message of the folktale.

_____

_____

_____

_____

_____

_____

_____

_____

_____

Name _____

Read. Then, answer the questions.

Rainbow Crow: A Lenape Tale

Long ago, before there was man, the crow was the most beautiful bird in the world. His wings were made of rainbow feathers, and his voice was the sweetest ever heard.

Then one day, snow came to the forest for the first time ever. The animals thought little of it at first, but soon Mouse was completely buried. They had to stop the snow before it covered everyone. Rainbow Crow offered to fly to the Great Sky Spirit and ask him to stop the snow.

Rainbow Crow flew high toward the spirits for three days. At last, he reached the Great Sky Spirit and asked him to stop the snow. The Great One said that he could not grant his request because the snow had its own spirit. He offered the gift of fire to warm the earth instead. He gave the bird a flaming stick to carry in his mouth back to the forest.

Rainbow Crow flew quickly toward Earth. On the first day, sparks from the flame burned his tail feathers, but he bravely flew on. The next day, he noticed his wing feathers were covered with black soot. On the third day, Rainbow Crow could barely breathe from the fire burning his throat, but he reached the woods just in time. His friends were completely buried now, so Rainbow Crow used the flame to melt the snow.

Crow looked at himself. He was no longer beautiful, and his voice had become cracked and raspy. Crow began to cry. The Great Sky Spirit appeared to him. He explained that one day man would come to Earth and hunt animals. He gave Crow the gift of freedom. "Man will not want your meat or your plain black feathers," he said. "But, you will always know your true beauty. Look closely at your feathers, for you will see all the colors of the rainbow reflecting in them." Crow returned to his friends in the forest, feeling proud, brave, and beautiful.

1. Why was Rainbow Crow "the most beautiful bird in the world"?

_____

2. How did Crow's good deed change him?

_____

3. Crow changes from being upset to "feeling proud, brave, and beautiful." Why?

_____

⚡ Reflect

What is the main idea of the fable? Explain how Rainbow Crow's changes support the main idea.

_____

_____

_____

Name _____

Read. Then, answer the questions on page 21.

The Snow Maiden

Many years ago, there lived an old man and an old woman. As they grew older, they also grew sadder, for they had no children.

One winter morning, the old man looked out the window at the falling snow. "Let's build a snow child," he suggested to his wife.

"Yes," said the old woman, "a snow maiden just for us."

The old man and the old woman went outside and began to make a little girl out of snow. They made her legs, her arms, and her head. They used bits of sparkling blue ice for her eyes. When the old man and old woman had finished, they stood back to look at what they had created. They could hardly believe their eyes. They had created a beautiful snow maiden. The old woman kissed the snow maiden gently on the cheek. Suddenly, the snow maiden began to smile. She stretched out her arms. Then, she stretched out her legs. She spun around and gave a little laugh. "I'm alive," she giggled with delight. Then, she ran and gave the old man and the old woman a hug. Nothing could have made the couple happier. At last, they had the child they had longed for.

The days passed. Soon, the winter storms turned to spring showers. The sun began to warm the earth. The signs of spring were everywhere. But, as the days became warmer, the snow maiden became more and more unhappy. She would not go outside. "Come, little daughter. Why do you look so sad? Go outside and play with the other children," said the old woman to the snow maiden. The snow maiden did as she was told.

But, before the snow maiden could join the other children, she disappeared. There was only a white mist where the girl had stood. The mist formed into a thin cloud and rose higher and higher until it joined the clouds in the sky. The old man and the old woman wept **bitterly** at the loss of their dear little snow maiden. Once again, they were sad and lonely.

After many months, the days became shorter and the nights longer. The air was crisp and cool once again. Winter was coming. One night, as the first snow began to fall, the couple sat by the window remembering their dear little snow maiden. Suddenly, they heard a happy laugh and a familiar voice singing,

Winter is here. I am back with the snow.
Do not fear, when in the spring I go.
For I will return with the snow each year
For you my parents are oh, so dear.

The couple ran to the door. They hugged their little snow maiden. How happy they were to be together again! The snow maiden stayed with them through each winter. Then, when spring came, she would disappear until winter returned to the old couple's cottage again.

Name _____

Read the story on page 20. Then, answer the questions.

1. Why are the old man and old woman sad?

_____

2. How do they choose to solve their problem?

_____

3. Why does the snow maiden become sad? How do you know?

_____

_____

4. Why does the snow maiden sing a song to the couple?

_____

_____

5. What does the word *bitterly* mean? How does it describe how the old couple felt about the loss of the snow maiden?

_____

_____

_____

Reflect

The snow maiden calls the old couple her *parents*. Why does the author use this word, even though she is not a normal child?

_____

_____

_____

_____

_____

_____

_____

Name _____

Read. Then, answer the questions.

The Roller Coaster

The roller coaster's like a snake,
  coiling 'round and 'round.
As the cars make their way up,
  my heart begins to pound.

The big drop comes so quickly,
  I can't scream or yell.
The whipping of the curves
  swings me like a bell.

As the ride comes to an end,
  I start to smile and laugh.
I shout, "Let's go again
  along that whipping path."

1. What words are repeated twice in the poem to describe the roller coaster?

_____

2. How would the poem be different if the author had used *curvy* instead?

_____

_____

3. What words and phrases does the author use to describe the curviness of the roller coaster?

_____

_____

Reflect

Based on the author's choice of words, did the author enjoy the roller coaster? Explain.

_____

_____

_____

_____

_____

_____

Name _____

Read. Then, answer the questions.

Teach Me

Don't tell me that I can't, or I won't.
Always tell me to try, and I will.

Teach me to smile when I am sad.
Teach me to talk when I am mad.

Teach me to soar, and teach me to fly.
Answer my questions when I ask why.

Teach me that failures are successes not tried.
Teach me to open my arms up wide.

Teach me to love and to laugh and to live.
Teach me to work and to share and to give.

Teach me so that I become all I can be.
Then, stand back and be proud of me.

1. What kinds of things does the author want to be taught?

_____

_____

2. What does the phrase "failures are successes not tried" mean?

_____

_____

3. Why does the author want to be taught all of these things?

_____

_____

Reflect

Who is the author writing to? Use evidence from the text to support your answer.

_____

_____

_____

_____

Name _____

Read. Then, answer the questions.

The Turtle
When traveling far it becomes quite a hurdle,
Deciding where you will sleep.
But, when you're a turtle with a shell for a girdle,
Your hotel room comes quite cheap.

Elephant
The elephant carries a great big trunk;
He never packs it with clothes.
It has no lock, and it has no key,
So he takes it wherever he goes.

Roadrunner
Roadrunner is quite different—
He likes to take a tan.
When running on hot desert roads,
I think I'd need a fan.

His cuckoo family members fly,
But, Runner hits the road.
I don't know who is kookier,
Or what's the better mode.

1. In "The Turtle," what does the author mean by "your hotel room comes quite cheap"?

   _____

2. In "Roadrunner," the author states that Runner "hits the road." What does it mean to *hit the road*? How does that phrase show the difference between Runner and the cuckoos?

   _____

   _____

3. In "Elephant," the word *trunk* has more than one meaning. Give each meaning and describe why the author used both meanings.

   _____

   _____

   _____

⁂ Reflect

Describe the common theme between all of the poems. Use evidence from the poems to support your answer.

_____

_____

_____

Name _____

Read. Then, answer the questions.

The Wind

Robert Louis Stevenson

I saw you toss the kites on high
And blow the birds about the sky;
And all around I heard you pass,
Like ladies' skirts across the grass—
    O wind, a-blowing all day long,
    O wind, that sings so loud a song!

I saw the different things you did,
But always you yourself you hid.
I felt you push, I heard you call,
I could not see yourself at all—
    O wind, a-blowing all day long,
    O wind, that sings so loud a song!

O you that are so strong and cold,
O blower, are you young or old?
Are you a beast of field and tree,
Or just a stronger child than me?
    O wind, a-blowing all day long,
    O wind, that sings so loud a song!

1. In what ways does the narrator notice the wind?

_____

_____

_____

2. Circle the lines that are repeated in each stanza.

3. What loud song does the wind sing?

_____

_____

☀ Reflect

What puzzles the narrator about the wind?

_____

_____

_____

Name _____

Read. Then, answer the questions on page 27.

If

If fairy tales were real,
How strange life would be!

We'd make three wishes
And talk to fishes.
How strange life would be!

We'd play checkers with Snow White,
Follow pebbles in the night.
How strange life would be!

We'd kiss frogs and slay dragons,
Ride in coaches and wagons.
How strange life would be!

If fairy tales were real,
We'd have porridge at every meal.
How strange life would be!

The magic is nice,
But I'd think twice
About living my life in a tale—

Or, I might just find
Myself in a bind
And living my life in a whale!

Fairy Tales

Come, read with me a fairy tale;
Board my ship and let's set sail.

Let's go to once upon a time,
Where good is good and all words rhyme.

Come, follow me to places afar,
beyond the moon, beyond a star.

We'll travel to lands so far away,
Where elves and fairies hide and play.

We'll pretend to be pirates who wander
   the sea,
Seeking adventure, wild and free.

Let's go where things are not as they seem,
To places we can only dream.

Name _____

Read the poems on page 26. Then, answer the questions.

1. In the poem "If," what line does the author repeat in each of the first five stanzas?

_____

2. How does the author of "If" feel about fairy tales? Explain how the repeated line helps you understand the author's point of view about fairy tales.

_____

_____

_____

3. In the poem "Fairy Tales," what adjectives does the author use?

_____

4. How does the author of "Fairy Tales" feel about fairy tales? Explain how the author's choice of words helps you understand the author's point of view about fairy tales.

_____

_____

_____

Reflect

Compare and contrast how the authors of "If" and "Fairy Tales" feel about fairy tales. Which poem do you prefer? Why?

_____

_____

_____

_____

_____

_____

_____

_____

_____

Name _____

Read. Then, answer the questions.

Animals' Sleeping Habits

Sleep for humans almost always means a bed or a mat is present. Animals, however, have many different ways of sleeping.

For warmth, some animals sleep in groups. Lions, monkeys, and penguins are a few of the animals that sleep in groups. Elephants also sleep in a group, but they sleep in groups for protection. The larger elephants make a circle around the younger elephants. The larger elephants sleep standing up, while the younger ones lie down to sleep.

Some animals sleep in trees. Birds will lock their feet onto a branch to keep from falling out of the tree. Other animals, like squirrels, make nests in the trees to sleep in.

Most animals look for dry places to sleep. However, ducks often sleep in water. So do sea otters. They float on their backs wrapped in seaweed to keep from floating away.

Most animals lie down to sleep. However, some large animals, like horses, can sleep standing up. The flamingo sleeps standing on just one leg.

Most animals sleep at night, but some animals are nocturnal. Nocturnal animals sleep during the day. Bats and owls are nocturnal animals. They wake up when the sun goes down.

Animals sleep in many different places and in many different ways. But, just like humans, every animal must sleep.

1. What is the main idea of the passage?

_____

2. How is the information organized?

_____

3. Compare and contrast how animals and humans sleep, based on the passage.

_____

_____

_____

☀ Reflect

What would you title this passage? Why? Support your choice with evidence from the passage.

_____

_____

_____

Name _____

Read. Then, answer the questions.

The Egg-Laying Mammal

When people in England first saw a stuffed platypus, they thought it was a joke. They thought someone had put a duck's bill on a beaver's body! Then, they saw other strange things. The platypus had webbed feet. It had short legs like a lizard's. It had two layers of fur. And, it had a spur on each of its back legs. What kind of animal was this?

The platypus lives in Australia. It is one of the strangest animals in the world. For one thing, it lays eggs, even though it is a mammal. It lives underground, but it spends a lot of time in the water. A platypus dives in the water up to 80 times an hour to get food. Its webbed feet and flat tail help it swim. It carries food in its cheeks until it is ready to eat. The platypus does not have teeth. It has little pads inside its bill that grind its food.

This furry brown animal is about the size of a house cat. It lives 10 to 17 years. Its babies are called **puggles**. The mother platypus feeds them milk after they hatch. They live in a burrow that is built with long tunnels.

Only the male platypus has spurs that it uses like stingers. It uses its spurs in fighting. When another animal is stung, it can die. Humans do not die from the sting of a platypus. But, they do get very sick. People in Australia learned to leave this odd animal alone!

1. Why did people in England think the platypus was a joke? Use information from the text and illustration to support your answer.

   _____

   _____

2. What are *puggles*?

   _____

3. How do you think the term *puggle* affects the platypus's reputation as a strange animal?

   _____

   _____

☀ Reflect

How does the author feel about the platypus? Use evidence from the text to support your answer. How can the author's opinion affect the reader?

_____

_____

Read. Then, answer the questions.

Don't Bug Me

Have you ever had a mosquito bite? If you were bitten by a mosquito, that mosquito was a female. Only female mosquitoes bite. They need your blood to make their eggs. Male mosquitoes just eat plant juices. Females eat plant juices, too, but they also need blood in their diets.

Animal blood and human blood contain protein. Mosquito eggs need that protein in order to be healthy and hatch. When the mosquito has gathered enough blood, she is ready to lay her eggs. So when she bites you, she is ensuring that there are more mosquitoes born.

When a mosquito bites, she is actually poking your skin with her **proboscis**, a long, thin tube that forms a mosquito's mouth. Your blood normally starts to thicken, or clot, as soon as it leaves your body—this is an important part of healing. However, a tiny mosquito does not want the blood she sucks to clot in her proboscis, so she spits a chemical while she bites. The chemical keeps your blood from clotting in her proboscis. Most people are allergic to this chemical. Their bodies react to the chemical by swelling, getting red, and itching. Some people are more sensitive than others.

Female mosquitoes are pretty annoying. They whine in our ears and take our blood. Then, they leave behind an itchy reminder wherever they bite.

1. Why does the author use the pronoun *she* throughout the passage?

_____

2. Why do only female mosquitoes bite humans?

_____

_____

3. What is a *proboscis*? How does it affect humans?

_____

_____

_____

⁂ Reflect

Does the author have an opinion about mosquitoes? If so, what is it? Use evidence from the passage to support your answer.

_____

_____

_____

Name _____

Read. Then, answer the questions.

Sea Horses

Sea horses are interesting creatures for many reasons. Their scientific name is *Hippocampus*. It comes from two Greek words: *hippos*, which means "horse," and *kampos*, which means "sea monster." To survive in the ocean, sea horses live in environments that camouflage them from predators. Sea horses range in size from 6–12 inches (15.2–30.5 cm), although most are about 6 inches long. They can be many colors, including white, yellow, red, brown, black, and gray, with spots or stripes. However, the most interesting thing about sea horses is that they put a twist on parenting. Instead of females carrying the young, males carry them!

A male sea horse has a pouch on his underside where he carries eggs. The female sea horse places her eggs into the male's pouch. Then, the male sea horse carries the eggs for about 21 days until they hatch. The female sea horse visits the male sea horse every morning until the babies are born. Newborn sea horses rise to the surface of the water and take a gulp of air, which helps them stay upright.

When sea horses are born, they use their snouts to feed on tiny creatures, using their snouts. They are able to swim, but sometimes they get washed up onshore by storms or eaten by fish, crabs, or waterbirds.

A few days after giving birth, the male joins the female again. Within hours, he has a new sack full of eggs. This is the life cycle of the sea horse. Sea horses are indeed interesting animals!

1. What makes sea horses different from most other animals?

_____

2. What topic about sea horses does the author focus on most in the passage?

_____

3. The author states several times that sea horses are "interesting" animals. What evidence is provided to support this claim?

_____

_____

☀ Reflect

Bias is when somebody has a clear opinion about a topic. Is the author of this passage biased? Why or why not? Does this affect the opinion of the reader?

_____

_____

_____

Name _____

Read. Then, answer the questions.

A Dinosaur Named Sue

What weighs 7 tons (6,350 kg), stands 13 feet tall, and is 67 million years old? Sue the Dinosaur. Sue's skeleton was found in the summer of 1990. Sue was a *Tyrannosaurus rex*. A fossil hunter named Sue Hendrickson found the skeleton.

Hendrickson and her team were digging near the Black Hills in Faith, South Dakota. Her team went into town to fix a flat tire. Hendrickson decided to stay to look for fossils. She saw some bone pieces on the ground. Then, she found more bones in a nearby cliff. She climbed up the cliff for a better look. There she saw the biggest *Tyrannosaurus rex* ever found. Her teamed named the dinosaur "Sue" in her honor.

The first *T. rex* skeleton was found around 1900. Since then, only seven more have been unearthed that were more than half complete. Sue is the largest, most complete, and best preserved *T. rex* ever found. They dug up over 200 of her bones.

It took about three weeks to remove Sue from the cliff. Then, it took years to clean the bones at a museum. Scientists can learn a lot about dinosaurs from Sue. The one thing they may never know is whether Sue was really a male or female.

Sue is now on display at the Field Museum in Chicago, Illinois. Two copies of the skeleton travel around the United States. Maybe you'll see Sue at a museum near you!

1. Why is the dinosaur named Sue?

_____

2. What makes Sue stand apart from the other *T. rex* skeletons that have been found?

_____

_____

3. Why is Sue so important to scientists? Use evidence from the text to support your answer.

_____

_____

☀ Reflect

Why does the author end the passage by telling readers that Sue may be at a museum near them?

_____

_____

_____

Name _____

Read. Then, answer the questions on page 34.

The Leopard That Went for Help

Billy Arjan Singh is a wildlife expert. He lives on a farm in India. At his home across the river from a big forest, he takes in orphans. These orphans have four legs and whiskers!

Billy works with big cats, like leopards and tigers.

One orphan cub was a leopard named Harriet. From the first day, Billy started to teach Harriet how to go back and live in the wild. He built tree platforms to teach her how to climb. He took her on walks in the forest and showed her how to hunt.

Finally, Harriet learned her lessons about living in the wild. She was ready to go live in the forest. Billy rowed Harriet across the river to the trees where she went into the forest on her own. Billy thought that he would never see her again.

He was wrong.

Floods came to the forest. Harriet and her cubs were in danger. Harriet remembered the place where she had been safe as a cub. She took her two cubs one by one across the river to Billy's house.

They stayed there until the floodwaters started to go down.

Harriet watched the river every day. One day, Harriet swam across the river and went to see her den. She decided that her den was safe again. She took the first cub across the river. But, the current in the river was strong, and she had trouble swimming.

Harriet asked for help. She took her cub in her mouth. She walked down to Billy's boat. She jumped in. Then, she stood there and waited for Billy to see her in the boat. When he did, he knew right away that Harriet was asking for a ride across the river.

Billy rowed Harriet and her cub across the river to the forest. She and her cubs went back to live in the wild again.

Billy still lives on the farm and he still helps animals. He once said in an interview that Harriet was the love of his life. Her trust in Billy was like a bridge between wild animals and humans.

Read the passage on page 33. Then, answer the questions.

1. Who is Harriet?

_____

2. How did Harriet first have contact with humans?

_____

_____

3. After Billy dropped Harriet off in the forest, why did he think he would never see her again?

_____

_____

4. In what ways did Harriet communicate with Billy?

_____

_____

_____

5. The author compares Harriet's trust in Billy to a bridge. What does the author mean? Use evidence from the text to support your answer.

_____

_____

_____

Reflect

The author doesn't say what happens to Billy and Harriet after she returned to the wild. Do you think Billy and Harriet ever saw each other again? Use evidence from the text to support your answer.

_____

_____

_____

_____

_____

Name _____

Read. Then, answer the questions.

A Migration Observation

You would be lucky if you lived in Japan, Hawaii, or Mexico. Once a year, the Northern Pacific humpback whales travel to these countries from Alaska. They have their babies in the warm, shallow waters near the coasts.

The trip the whales make is called a **migration**. Humpback whales feed from June to October. Then, whales travel up to 4,000 miles (6,437km) each way to their breeding grounds.

The markings on the underside of each humpback whale's flukes are unique. A **fluke** is a tail fin and is like a whale's fingerprint. Scientists found out how fast the humpback whales can migrate by checking their flukes.

Humpback whales are as curious as cats. They will come right up to a boat full of people. People can see the whales doing tricks when they come to the surface to breathe. It is called "**spyhopping**" if the whale lifts one-third of its body out of the water. "**Lobtailing**" is when it slaps the water with its tail.

Everyone's favorite trick is when a whale **breaches**. Its entire body—40–50 feet (12.2–15.2 meters) long and weighing 25–40 tons (22,680–36,287 kilograms)—comes up out of the water. Then, it crashes back down with a giant belly flop. The noise is like thunder.

Humpback whales make the best noise when they sing. They can't sing like people do. They have no vocal cords, and no air is blown out. No one knows for sure how they sing. Some scientists think air circles around inside tubes in the whales' bodies to make the noise. One song can last up to 30 minutes.

Maybe one day you will get to see a humpback whale or hear its song!

1. What is the purpose of the bolded words throughout the passage?

_____

_____

2. What other animal does the author compare humpback whales to? Why?

_____

_____

3. When are people and scientists able to observe humpback whales?

_____

_____

🔆 Reflect

The passage is titled "A Migration Observation," even though the author only mentions the whales' migration in the first two paragraphs. Why did the author choose that title?

_____

_____

Name _____

Read. Then, answer the questions on page 37.

Driver Ants: All for One

Ants can be found almost anywhere on Earth. Over 8,000 kinds of ants have been discovered. Ants look the same today as they did when dinosaurs were alive. Scientists found some ants from that time preserved in amber, which is fossilized tree sap. It hardened with the ants stuck inside. The old ants look just like ants do now.

Most ants live in colonies. A colony has one very large queen, and she lays all of the eggs. Most ants are females, but most don't lay eggs. Every ant in a colony has a special job.

Driver Ant Colonies

One of the most remarkable ants of all lives in Africa. It is called the driver ant. There can be over 20 million driver ants in one colony.

In a driver ant colony, there are soldier ants that have large **mandibles**, or jaws. Solider ants protect the queen and the workers. But, soldier ants cannot feed themselves because of their large mandibles. It is the job of smaller worker ants to get food and feed the queen and the soldier ants.

Ant Food

Driver ants are **carnivorous**, which means that they eat meat. They will eat anything that cannot get away. Sometimes, they eat large animals like cows. However, driver ants mostly eat frogs, spiders, and insects like cockroaches and praying mantises. Driver ant colonies can capture more than 100,000 other insects per day.

People who live in the jungle move out of their huts and villages when they hear that driver ants are coming. After the ants are gone, villagers come back to a home that is free of insects.

Ants on the Move

Driver ants are **nomads**. They eat and then move on to find more food. Colonies travel from place to place and do not make permanent homes. If a queen is laying eggs, her colony stops for a short time. They make a nest out of their own bodies. Some ants form walls, and others form the ceiling. When the babies, which are called **grubs**, can travel, the colony moves on.

Nothing stops driver ants on the move. A colony works well as a team. The ants can build a bridge by climbing and holding onto each other until they reach the other side of a stream. Driver ant colonies have been known to form balls and float on water. What great cooperation!

Name _____

Read the passage on page 36. Then, answer the questions.

1. The passage states that each ant in a colony has a special job. What are some examples of the jobs ants may have?

_____

2. What subheading helped you find the answer to question 1?

_____

_____

3. What examples does the author provide to show how driver ants work together?

_____

_____

_____

4. How do the mandibles of soldier ants help the colony? How do they force the soldiers to rely on other ants?

_____

_____

_____

5. How does the final sentence relate to the main idea of the passage?

_____

_____

_____

☀ Reflect

How does the title support the main idea of the passage? Use details and evidence from the passage to support your answer.

_____

_____

_____

_____

_____

_____

Name _____

Read. Then, answer the questions.

Paper Towels

Do you know that many inventions were accidents? Sometimes, new ideas come to people when they are working on something else. Paper towels were invented because of a mistake. The Scott Paper Company made the first paper towels. They weren't out looking for a better towel. The paper towel just showed up at their factory one day.

The Scott Paper Company made toilet paper. They ordered the fine tissue in long rolls from a paper mill. Then, they cut the rolls into the right size and packaged them for home use.

Unfortunately, one day a shipment came from the paper mill that was all wrong. The tissue was too thick and wrinkled. The buyers were ready to send the wrong paper back, when someone had an idea. He said that the thick paper would make nice hand towels that people could use once and then throw away.

The Scott Paper Company **perforated** the rolls of thick paper so that they would tear into towel-sized pieces. They packaged the paper rolls and sold them in stores as "Sani-Towels."

Instead of sending the mistake back, Scott Paper Company created a new product that still sells well over 100 years later. So you see, mistakes can be a great learning experience if you can think in a new way.

1. What does *perforated* mean?

_____

2. How was the invention of the paper towel an accident?

_____

_____

3. Usually inventions are created and perfected by people. How was the invention of the paper towel different?

_____

_____

⁂ Reflect

What lesson could a reader learn from this passage? Use evidence from the passage to support your answer.

_____

_____

_____

Name _____

Read. Then, answer the questions.

Chewing Gum

My name is Thomas Adams. You probably have no idea who I am, but I invented chewing gum. Well, invented might be a strong word.

I lived in the 1800s. I once met General Santa Anna. He was a Mexican general. Santa Anna told me about a dried sap called chicle. He liked to chew this sap that came from the sapodilla tree. He said that Mayans and others had been chewing it for hundreds of years. I tried some. Honestly, I thought it tasted terrible.

But, I was interested in chicle because it was so rubbery. Maybe I could make things like toys or boots from it. But, nothing seemed to work. It wasn't going to replace rubber.

One day, I popped a terrible-tasting piece of chicle in my mouth and chewed and chewed. Yuck, I thought. Wouldn't it be nice if it had some flavor? Eureka! I had a great idea! I opened a flavored-gum factory and sold chewing gum like crazy.

Americans loved my gum. But, doctors seemed to think it was bad. They said it was bad for your teeth. Well, that may be true, but one doctor even said, "Chewing gum will exhaust the salivary glands and cause intestines to stick together." Isn't that the silliest thing you have ever heard?

I am proud to say that flavored chewing gum was a hit! But, why doesn't anyone know my name?

1. Who discovered chewing chicle?

_____

2. What did Thomas Adams do to chicle to create chewing gum?

_____

3. Look at the first and last paragraphs. How does the author feel about Thomas Adams being forgotten?

_____

_____

☀ Reflect

This passage is written as if Thomas Adams were talking to the audience. Underline words and phrases that are usually only used when talking. How would the passage be different if it had been written using formal English?

_____

_____

_____

_____

Read. Then, answer the questions.

A Sea without Fish

Water in the middle of a desert sounds good. But, the Dead Sea does not hold water that people or animals can drink. The Dead Sea is the saltiest place on Earth. It is really a lake. It is called a sea because it does not have freshwater.

Why is the Dead Sea so salty? It sits almost a quarter mile (0.4 km) below sea level. More than three million years ago, salt water from the Mediterranean Sea went into the Dead Sea. Water flows into the Dead Sea today from a river. The water has no outlet. Some of the water evaporates in the hot sun. Salt is left behind.

Scientists say that the Dead Sea is sinking. It has sunk as much as 13 inches (33.02 cm) in some years. People are using more water from the river. Less freshwater enters the lake every year.

Lakes are usually filled with plants and animals. But, the Dead Sea lives up to its name. Nothing can stay alive there. There is no seaweed. No birds or animals can drink its salty water. If fish from the river swim into the Dead Sea by mistake, they die quickly. The water kills almost everything. It is at least seven times saltier than ocean water.

People like to visit this lake. There are hotels and beaches. People float in the Dead Sea. The salty water holds people's bodies up as if they were lying on rafts! It is actually harder to stand in the Dead Sea than it is to float. Some tourists even like to read books as they float on top of the water. When they come out, they are covered with salt.

1. Why is the body of water named the Dead Sea?

_____

2. What causes the Dead Sea to be so salty?

_____

_____

3. How is the Dead Sea like a lake? How is it different?

_____

_____

☀ Reflect

Why did the author give the passage the title "A Sea without Fish"? Use evidence from the passage to support your answer.

_____

_____

_____

Name _____

Read. Then, answer the questions.

A City Survives

Would you build a house on an island made of sand? What if the sand was only a few feet above sea level? Well, that is just what 37,000 people did in the 1800s. That island city is Galveston, Texas.

Many people had said the island was safe. There had been a few storms before that didn't do much harm. So, people kept coming and building. Then, on September 8, 1900, something bad happened.

A huge hurricane hit the island. Many people went to the mainland across a bridge. Then, the bridge was underwater too. Thousands more people had to stay on the island.

The winds were blowing at about 120 miles (193 km) per hour. Most of the homes and buildings were gone. The entire island was underwater. But, the water kept rising.

Finally, at dawn, the storm was over. The survivors couldn't believe what they saw. More than 6,000 people died, but over 30,000 people lived.

The hurricane was one of the worst natural disasters in United States history. But, the people of Galveston wouldn't give up. They used what they learned and rebuilt their island city. They also built a seawall. It is 16 feet (4.88 m) high and 17 feet (5.18) thick. In the year 2012, over 47,000 people called Galveston their home.

1. The hurricane of September 8, 1900 is called, "one of the worst natural disasters in United States history." Why? Use evidence from the text to support your answer.

   _____

   _____

   _____

2. What happened as a direct result of the hurricane?

   _____

   _____

3. The author writes the article *chronologically*, or in the order that events happened. Underline the clues in the article that show that the article is chronological.

☀ Reflect

The author uses foreshadowing in the second paragraph by hinting that "something bad happened." How would the article be different if foreshadowing were not used?

_____

_____

Name _____

Read. Then, answer the questions.

Setting a Record

Roy C. Sullivan was hit by lightning seven times. That is a world record. Each year in the US, about 95 people die from lightning strikes. Lightning can also cause some bad injuries. Roy lost a toenail and burned both eyebrows. His hair was once set on fire. He also had scars on his shoulder, chest, stomach, ankle, and leg.

Roy became a serious weather watcher. He knew all about lightning. He knew that you can't outrun it. A bolt of lightning can travel over 60,000 miles per second (96,561 km per second). Lightning can even run underground. It can travel many feet from where it touched down.

There are some steps you can take to protect yourself from lightning. First, pay attention to weather reports before going outside. As soon as you see lightning or hear thunder, find a nearby building. If you're not close to a building, get in a car, if possible. If you can't do either, then move away from tall things that lightning is more likely to strike, such as trees or flagpoles. Stay away from open fields or water. You should sit down or lay flat on the ground. This way you won't be the tallest thing in the area. That may feel silly, but it could save your life.

Roy Sullivan never wanted to set a record. He knew that being hit by lightning is bad news. He was a very lucky man.

1. What record does the title of the passage refer to?

_____

2. How did Sullivan react to being struck by lightning so often?

_____

_____

3. What is the main idea of the passage?

_____

_____

☀ Reflect

One paragraph in the passage does not focus on Sullivan. Identify the paragraph and explain why the author included it.

_____

_____

_____

Name _____

Read. Then, answer the questions on page 44.

Eight Minutes over France

Do you like to travel in different ways? Then, try going by hot air balloon. The idea existed for 2,000 years. But, it took the king of France, two brothers, a sheep, a duck, and a chicken to make it happen 1783.

The king of France thought a person would die traveling by balloon. So, two brothers did a test. They sent the three animals up in a basket attached to a balloon.

The animals flew over France for eight minutes. The king was excited when they returned safely. Two months later, a major in the army and a physics professor went up in a balloon.

A hot air balloon is so simple, it seems anyone could fly one. Turning a knob lets gas into the balloon. This makes the balloon go up. Pulling a cord changes the amount of gas and makes the balloon rise quickly or slowly. If the cord lets enough gas out, the balloon sinks. The wind moves the balloon from place to place.

In the 1960s, hot air balloons became very popular. A man named Ed Yost worked with Raven Industries to design and make hot air balloons. Then, the United States Navy asked Ed's company to help them. The navy wanted to use balloons to send packages.

Ed Yost and the navy made important changes. Balloons were made from a new material. The balloon's shape was made to look like a giant light bulb.

Someone also invented of a new way to inflate the balloon. Now, just the top part of the balloon is filled. Some safety changes were also made. It is safer than ever to travel by hot air balloon.

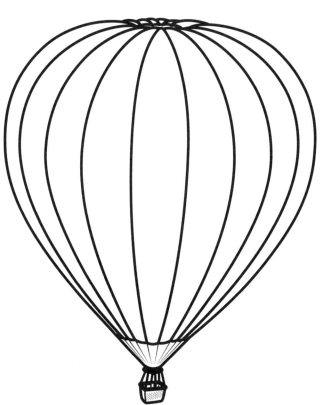

After a while, the navy lost interest in hot air balloons. But, Ed Yost didn't give up. He sold hot air balloons for sports events.

Hot air balloon businesses make millions of dollars. Balloon races attract crowds of spectators. Many people take part in the fun.

Some people have traveled around the world in balloons. Once you try it, you will never want to fly any other way.

Name _____

Read the passage on page 43. Then, answer the questions.

1. Why did people not travel by balloon 2,000 years ago?

_____

_____

2. What does the title of the passage refer to?

_____

_____

3. How are those eight minutes important to the history of hot air balloons? Use evidence from the text to support your answer.

_____

_____

_____

4. How was Ed Yost important to the history of hot air balloons?

_____

_____

_____

Reflect

Look at the title of the passage. The event it refers to is only a small part of the whole passage. Why did the author choose to name the passage this?

_____

_____

_____

_____

_____

_____

_____

_____

Name _____

Read. Then, answer the questions on page 46.

Stars on Earth

Some people are looking up at a group of low hills in West Texas. Suddenly, they see glowing, reddish-orange lights. Are they the headlights of cars on the highway? Are they the lights of campfires? The people shout and point. The lights are moving! But, they aren't moving the way cars move. They go up in the air. They fall back to the earth. And then they simply disappear!

Every night, people go to look at the famous Marfa lights. They are named for the town of Marfa, Texas. The lights can be seen east of the town when you look at the hills in the distance. There have been many ideas about these strange lights over the years. One **theory** is that the lights are the headlights of cars driving down the road.

But, that could not be true. Settlers in the 1880s wrote about the lights. That was long before there were cars with headlights. At that time, pioneers thought the Marfa lights were the campfires of Apaches in the hills. When they would ride into the hills, they could not find evidence of campsites or fires. Later, the settlers learned that the Apaches, too, could see the lights. They said the lights were stars that had come down to Earth.

Some people say that the lights are moonlight shining on minerals in the hills. Others say they are made by gas from swamps. Some scientists have tried to prove that the lights really are light from planets or stars. They say that the lights reflect in a strange way on the hills. That doesn't help us understand why the lights can "dance." They move up and down, slow down, and speed up. These dancing "stars," the Marfa lights, stay a mystery.

Name _____

Read the passage on page 45. Then, answer the questions.

1. Describe the Marfa lights and why they are considered so strange.

_____

_____

2. What is a *theory*?

_____

3. What theories do people have about the Marfa lights?

_____

_____

_____

4. Stars are mentioned twice in the passage. Which groups of people believed the Marfa lights are stars? How are the theories of those groups different?

_____

_____

_____

☀ Reflect

What does it mean when the passage says the Marfa lights "stay a mystery"? Why did the author end the passage with that phrase?

_____

_____

_____

_____

_____

_____

_____

_____

_____

Name _____

Read. Then, answer the questions.

A Cold Place

Verkhoyansk, Russia, is one of the coldest places in the northern hemisphere. The little town of 1,800 people is in Siberia. On its coldest winter day on record, the temperature was -90°F (-67.78°C)!

What is life there like in the winter? In winter, a whooshing sound can be heard. It sounds like rice being poured out of a bag. It is the sound of people's breath turning into ice crystals. The crystals fall to the ground in front of them.

The cold makes life difficult. It is so cold that trees can explode and houses can split. If people drink hot tea, their teeth can crack. And, if people go outside and pour the tea out of their cups, it can freeze before it hits the ground.

Winter there is dark, as well as cold. On some days, the only daylight is a low, faint light. You may think that no one would want to live in such a cold place. In the past, the town was used as a prison. People were sent to live there as punishment!

But, other people are from tribes who have lived there for thousands of years. There are groups of nomads who live in the mountains. They say that it is actually warmer in the mountains than it is in the town! That is because the town is in a **valley** between the mountains. The coldest air comes into the valley, and the mountains hold it there.

People there have found ways to deal with the cold. They melt blocks of ice from the river on the stove for water. They buy their milk in frozen disks. It is easy to carry the milk home and melt the disks when they are needed. That's life in Verkhoyansk!

1. What is a *valley*?

_____

2. How does being in a valley affect the town of Verkhoyansk?

_____

_____

3. What is the main idea of the passage? Use details from the text to support your answer.

_____

_____

🔆 Reflect

The author uses several exclamation points. How would the passage be different if periods were used instead?

_____

_____

Read. Then, answer the questions.

The History of the Bicycle

Did you know that a bicycle was once called a velocipede? The idea of a bike came from a child's toy, the hobbyhorse. A hobbyhorse had a horse's head on one end of a stick and a wheel on the other.

There have been many funny-looking bycycles. At first, bikes had no pedals. People made them go by pushing with their feet, like a scooter. Then, a blacksmith made the first pedals. Many of the bikes had a large front wheel that was turned by hand. People believed the large wheel would make the bike go faster. Most of the first bikes were made of wood and couldn't turn or stop.

Many new inventions helped make a better bicycle. For example, the front tire was made to turn and help steer. Also, early bikes had solid tires that made them bounce and shake. People had a nickname for bikes. They called them "boneshakers." Then, a man invented a new kind of tire. He put a hose on his son's tricycle and filled the hose with air. It helped stop the shaking. Another helpful invention was brakes. In time, bikes got lights, bells, and rearview mirrors.

Bicycles were not as popular for traveling once people started driving cars. Then, bike racing became a major sport. The Tour de France is the best example of bicycle racing. The bicycle is still a popular way to travel for people all over the world. And, it is much faster than walking!

1. What two odd names was the bicycle called?

_____

2. How has the bicycle changed over time?

_____

_____

3. What does the author blame for bicycles becoming less popular?

_____

Reflect

Is the bicycle shown in the illustration an old or modern bike? Explain how you know. How does the illustration help readers better understand the passage?

_____

_____

Name _____

Read. Then, answer the questions on page 50.

Chinese Immigrants

China is a very large country. Many people live in China. In the late 1800s, overcrowded towns and villages in China meant there wasn't much food. The Chinese people were paying most of the money they earned to the government. They couldn't earn enough money to care for their families. During this time, many Chinese men moved to America with dreams of wealth and **prosperity**.

The Chinese men discovered that America wasn't the "golden door" they expected. Many Americans in the west were digging for gold and striking it rich. The immigrants from China wanted to strike it rich too. But, the Chinese men weren't allowed to claim the gold. Some Americans would hire the Chinese men to dig for gold. They paid the Chinese men a very small salary, but they wouldn't let them have any rights to the gold. Many of the Chinese decided to start their own businesses, such as a laundry services, shops, and restaurants.

The women remained in China to take care of the children and the family-owned land. As the children grew older, the boys were sent to the United States to work with their fathers and grandfathers.

Ling-Shau Yu's Journal

June 15, 1926

I am so excited. I am going to go with my grandfather to the **New World**. I had to beg my mother to allow me to go. I want to see my father. He has been in the New World for two years. I wonder what it is like. I wonder why my father left us to go there.

June 20, 1926

This morning, I said good-bye to my mother, my grandmother, and my homeland, China. I will miss my family. I will miss China. My mother cried, and my grandmother went back inside the house. My grandfather and I got on a huge boat. It was the biggest boat I have ever seen. Many other people got on the boat too. We are all going to the New World. Grandfather says that the trip will be long. He says that I should be patient, but I can't. I want to be in the New World now. I want to see my father and help him with his new laundry business.

July 15, 1926

We have finally reached America. The boat trip was harder than I expected. I became sick, and I had to lie down most of the time. I miss my grandmother and mother. There are many people here. Everyone looks very different from people in my country. A doctor looked down my throat. Other people checked my paperwork and made my grandfather sign many papers. My grandfather told me to be polite. I tried to be polite, but it was hard. I want to see my father.

July 18, 1926

Today, I found my father. He was glad to see us. We hugged and we cried. It was good to be in his arms again. He took us to his home. It had two bedrooms. Grandfather got his own bedroom, and Father and I share a room. I do not have any more time to write. Father is taking us to his shop to work. It is good to be in the New World. It is good to be with my father. I hope that my mother and grandmother will join us soon.

Name _____

Read the passages on page 49. Then, answer the questions.

1. In the passage "Chinese Immigrants," what does *prosperity* mean?

_____

2. How does Ling-Shau Yu's feel about traveling to America? Is his experience similar to other Chinese immigrants? Give evidence from both passages to support your answer.

_____

_____

_____

3. Compare and contrast the information given about Chinese immigrants in both passages.

_____

_____

_____

4. One passage calls America the *golden door*. The other passage calls it the *New World*. Explain how these terms show how Chinese immigrants viewed America.

_____

_____

_____

☀ Reflect

The two passages present similar information in very different ways. One gives facts, and the other shows a personal account. How does each approach affect the reader differently?

_____

_____

_____

_____

_____

_____

_____

Name _____

Read. Then, answer the questions.

Benjamin Franklin

Benjamin Franklin was born in Boston on January 17, 1706. He was a printer, a statesman, and an inventor.

At the age of 15, Ben Franklin began working as a printer. By 1728, Franklin had opened his own printing office in Philadelphia. He printed newspapers and books. He wrote many of the things he printed. In 1733, Franklin wrote and published *Poor Richard's Almanack*. He also printed all of the money for the state of Pennsylvania.

Ben Franklin worked hard to make the colony of Pennsylvania a better place to be. He made improvements in the postal system and the police force. He established the first public library. He also helped start the first fire station after a fire destroyed much of the city of Philadelphia. He was elected delegate of Pennsylvania to the Second Continental Congress in 1775. In 1776, he helped write the Declaration of Independence.

Franklin was also an inventor. He was always thinking of ways to do things faster and better. In 1743, he invented a stove that would heat and stay at a certain temperature. He invented a type of eyeglasses that he could use to help him read in his old age. He is probably best known for the important discoveries he made with electricity in the early 1750s.

Benjamin Franklin died on April 17, 1790, at the age of 84. More than 20,000 people attended his funeral. He was an American hero who is still remembered today.

1. What is Benjamin Franklin probably best known for?

_____

2. What is the main idea of the passage?

_____

3. How do the three middle paragraphs support the main idea?

_____

_____

☀ Reflect

Why did the author choose to start the passage with Benjamin Franklin's birth and end with his death?

_____

_____

_____

_____

Read. Then, answer the questions on page 53.

Balancing Act

A little French boy named Jean François Gravelet went to the circus for the first time in 1829. He was five years old. He liked the horses and the clowns. Then, he saw a tightrope walker. He knew that was what he wanted to do. When he grew up, this little boy later took the **stage name** of Charles Blondin.

Charles's father sent him to a school for gymnasts. After his father passed away, Charles joined a circus to make his living. He was only nine years old. When he grew up, he went to the United States. On that trip, he saw Niagara Falls. It was just like the time when he first saw the tightrope walker. Charles knew that he had to cross the falls on a tightrope.

The great day was June 30, 1859. Charles's team put up a rope that was three inches (7.62 cm) thick and 1,100 feet (335.28 m) long. The rope sagged in the middle. It was close to 300 feet (91.44 m) above the falls! Many people came to watch this **feat**. No one had ever tried it before.

Charles made it across safely. He wanted to do more. He made more trips across Niagara Falls. Charles had new tricks to please the people. One time, he stood on a chair. Another time, he pushed a wheelbarrow across the rope. Charles even walked across the tightrope blindfolded. On one of his most amazing trips, he cooked some eggs on a small stove. Then, he ate them!

His trips across Niagara Falls made Charles famous. Later, he performed around Europe. He did not retire until he was 68 years old.

Name _____

Read the passage on page 52. Then, answer the questions.

1. What is a *stage name*? How do you know?

_____

_____

2. The author describes the time Charles sees Niagara Falls as "just like" when he saw a tightrope walker. What does the author mean?

_____

_____

3. What is a *feat*? What feats did Charles Blondin perform?

_____

_____

_____

4. What is the main idea of the passage? How does the illustration support the main idea?

_____

_____

_____

☀ Reflect

The author states that Charles did tricks to "please the people." How does the passage support this idea?

_____

_____

_____

_____

_____

_____

_____

Name _____

Read. Then, answer the questions.

The Violin as a Voice

Sarah Chang says that the violin is the closest music to the human voice. Sarah was three years old when she learned how to play violin. Her parents helped her learn to play. Sarah was only five years old when she was accepted into a famous music school called Juilliard. Her parents were amazed!

Sarah's father was her first teacher. He also plays violin. Sarah's mother is a **composer**, or someone who writes music. She helped Sarah learn how to read music.

Sarah's whole life has been about her talent. She started to play with orchestras when she was eight years old. At nine, she had recorded some of her music on CDs. A famous musician named Yehudi Menuhin said that Sarah was the most perfect violinist he had ever heard.

Sarah travels often to play with different orchestras. She says that her entire life is planned. Sometimes, she doesn't like that. She wishes that she had more free time. She says that if she doesn't touch a violin for a few days, her fingers start to miss playing. She also says she loves to be on the stage playing music for other people. For her, that's the most important thing in life.

1. In what ways is Sarah Chang special?

_____

_____

2. According to Sarah, what parts of her life does she enjoy? What parts does she not enjoy?

_____

_____

3. What does Sarah Chang compare violin music to? How does this support her feelings about the violin and making music?

_____

_____

Reflect

Look at the title of the passage. Describe how it relates to the main idea of the passage.

_____

_____

Name _____

Read. Then, answer the questions on page 56.

Nellie Bly

In 1889, a trip around the world was much harder than it is today. There were no jet airplanes or cars. There were only trains and ships. Also, women didn't travel alone much. They especially didn't travel around the world. Nellie Bly was a female journalist. Bly told her boss not to send a man instead of her. If he did, she would make the trip for another newspaper and beat the man. Her boss told her she could go. Nellie Bly was going on a trip around the world.

On November 14, 1889, Bly left New York City. She sailed away on a steamship called the *Augusta Victoria*. She only took one small handbag with her. Her only clothes were the ones she was wearing. On the very first night, a terrible storm rocked the ship. Bly was seasick. She wondered if she was doing the right thing. But, the world was watching. She couldn't turn back.

When Bly reached England, she was told that Jules Verne wanted to meet her. Bly was excited. To see the famous author, she traveled to France, losing two nights of sleep to stay on schedule.

After meeting Verne, she took a train through Italy. Then, she sailed on a ship to Egypt. From there, she rushed to the country of Yemen. Next, she traveled east to what is now Sri Lanka. Along the way, she wrote newspaper stories about the foods she ate, the clothes people wore, and the different cultures.

Thousands of people around the world read about Bly's trip in the papers. The newspaper even made a board game out of Bly's trip. A contest was held too. If someone could guess how long Bly's trip would last, that person would win a trip to Europe.

Bly reached San Francisco with 12 days left. She got on a train that sped across the country in 4 days. On January 25, 1890, she returned home to New York City and thousands of cheering fans. Bly had traveled around the world in only 72 days. It was a new world record!

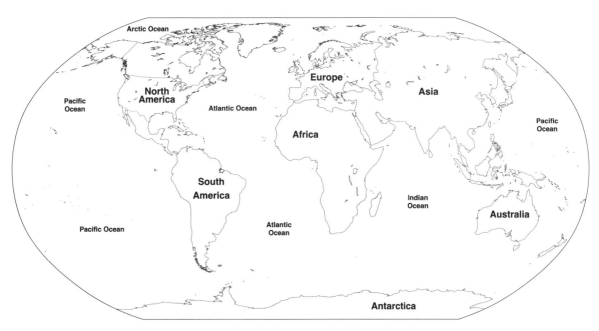

Name _____

Read the passage on page 55. Then, answer the questions.

1. Who was Nellie Bly?

_____

_____

2. Why was Bly's trip so rare?

_____

_____

3. The author follows a *chronological*, or time-based, format for the passage. List the important events in order.

_____

_____

_____

4. How did Bly's trip affect the world? Give examples from the passage.

_____

_____

_____

☀ Reflect

How would Nellie Bly's trip be the same and different if she did it today? Use details from the passage to support your answer.

_____

_____

_____

_____

_____

_____

_____

_____

_____

Read. Then, answer the questions.

Ty Cobb

Many people argue about whether Ty Cobb was the greatest baseball player of all time. But, everyone agrees that he was the meanest player of all time.

Ty Cobb played most of his 24-year professional career for the Detroit Tigers at the beginning of the 1900s. He was the game's fiercest competitor both on and off the field. His temper and attitude provoked injuries and fights with other players and sometimes even with his own teammates. Legend has it that Cobb sharpened his spikes before every game to intimidate and even injure other players. He firmly believed that he "owned" the base paths and often proclaimed that no opposing player was going to get in his way.

Cobb had good reason to believe that he did own the base paths. His stolen-base record of 96 in 1915 stood for 47 years. His batting accomplishments are also legendary. He had a lifetime average of .366. He hit 295 triples. He boasted 4,191 hits. He held 12 batting titles (including 9 in a row). Cobb played 23 straight seasons in which he hit over .300. During three of those seasons he hit over .400, topped by a .420 mark in 1911. His stats include 1,938 RBI, 2,245 runs, and the Triple Crown in 1909. Cobb led the league five times in stolen bases; his batting average was tops for nine consecutive years (1907–1915) and 12 times in all. He stole 892 bases in his 24 years at bat.

Ty Cobb, also known as "The Georgia Peach," was the first player elected into the Baseball Hall of Fame. He even beat out the legendary and popular Babe Ruth. When he retired, he "owned" virtually every hitting record that was kept. Although people love to hate Ty Cobb, he was a baseball player to remember.

1. What opinion does the author share in the first paragraph?

_____

2. What reasons does the author give to support the opinion?

_____

_____

3. What is the main idea of the passage?

_____

☀ Reflect

The third paragraph is different from all the others. How? Why did the author include such a different paragraph?

_____

_____

_____

Read. Then, answer the questions on page 59.

"A Challenge to Others"

Reporter: This is Mona Beck from WING radio. I am with Amelia Earhart in Miami, Florida. It is June 1, 1937. May I ask you some questions, Amelia?

Amelia: Yes, I have some time. They are getting the plane ready for our trip.

Reporter: Amelia, how did you feel when you saw a plane for the first time?

Amelia: I was at the Iowa State Fair. The plane I saw was made of wire and wood. It wasn't very exciting.

Reporter: Where did you live then?

Amelia: We were living in California, and our family was at an airplane show. It was there that I flew for the very first time. The ride lasted only 10 minutes, but I knew I wanted to learn to fly.

Reporter: When did you meet your husband, George Putnam?

Amelia: George was a New York publisher when we met. He asked me to be the first woman to fly across the Atlantic Ocean.

Reporter: Were you alone when you flew that time in 1928?

Amelia: Oh, no! I was not even flying the plane. I just rode along for that trip.

Reporter: Let's travel back to 1932. What happened in May of that year?

Amelia: I'm always looking for exciting things to do. Charles Lindbergh had flown solo across the Atlantic. That was something no one else had done. So, on May 20, 1932, I began the flight alone from Canada to England.

Reporter: But, your plane landed in a pasture in Ireland.

Amelia: Yes, the plane had flown a little off course. There was a man in the field watching the plane. He asked me if I had come a long way. I told him I had come from America. I had achieved George's goal.

Reporter: You are also the only person to fly across the Atlantic Ocean two times. President Roosevelt said you have shown that women can fly as well as men. Do you think you can set another record?

Amelia: It will be a challenge. Fred Noonan and I are planning to fly around the world. Fred will decide where we fly. He's my navigator.

Reporter: Good luck, Amelia! Have a safe trip.

Amelia: Thank you, Mona.

On June 1, 1937, everything was ready. Amelia and Fred Noonan left Florida flying the *Electra*. They were going to fly around the world.

On June 29, the plane was in New Guinea. They had flown 22,000 miles (35,406 km)! Amelia and Fred had only 7,000 miles (11,265 km) to go. But, this part of the trip was over the Pacific Ocean. July 2 was the last time anyone heard from them.

President Roosevelt asked for ships and planes to search the ocean. They searched for 16 days. They never found the two fliers.

Amelia had written a letter to George. In it, she wrote, "Women must try to do things as men have tried. When they fail, their failure must be a challenge to others."

Name _____

Read the passage on page 58. Then, answer the questions.

1. What records did Amelia Earhart set in her time?

_____

_____

2. How did Amelia's successes lead to her choice to try and fly around the world? Did anything else affect her choice?

_____

_____

_____

3. The title of the passage is "A Challenge to Others." It is taken from a letter Amelia Earhart wrote and is quoted in the last paragraph. Why did the author choose this as the title? Use evidence from the passage to support your answer.

_____

_____

_____

_____

Reflect

The author chose to end the passage with a quote from Amelia Earhart. What effect does this have on the passage? Think about how it affects the reader and how the passage would be different if it wasn't included.

_____

_____

_____

_____

_____

_____

_____

_____

Name _____

Read. Then, answer the questions on page 61.

Where Is Amelia?

Amelia Earhart flew airplanes at a time when women didn't do such things. She was the first woman to fly across the Atlantic Ocean. She made many daring trips. In 1937, Amelia planned to fly around the world. Instead, she **vanished**.

Most of her trip went well. She and her copilot, Fred Noonan, got to the Pacific Ocean. On July 2, 1937, they planned to fly to a tiny island. A ship was nearby. It was there to listen for Amelia's messages on the radio.

The day was supposed to be clear. It was not. The flight took longer than planned. Amelia sent a message to the ship. She said her plane was getting low on gas. Then, she said she could not see the island. By that time, the plane had very little gas left. Amelia said she would keep sending messages. After that, there was only silence.

The president of the United States called for a search. Over four million dollars was spent to try to find the lost pilot. Ships searched over 250,000 square miles (647,497 sq. km) of sea. The work lasted over two weeks. No clues were found.

At first, people thought that the plane had just run out of gas. It must have crashed into the sea. Then, Amelia's mother told reporters that her daughter may have planned her trip for the government. Other people said Amelia was looking for facts about ships from Japan. Was Amelia Earhart a spy?

The search still goes on for Amelia Earhart. Many people have looked for her airplane.

One person thought he had found her grave, but he had not. Other people have found parts of planes. They thought the parts were from the crash of Amelia's airplane. But, many planes crashed in the Pacific Ocean during World War II.

No proof has ever been found that Amelia was a spy. Her body and her plane have never been found. We may never know the whole story about this great pilot. She is gone, but her story lives on.

Name _____

Read the passage on page 60. Then, answer the questions.

1. What does *vanished* mean?

_____

2. How would the meaning change if the author stated "Instead, she *was lost*," instead of *vanished*?

_____

_____

_____

3. What possible reasons does the author provide for Earhart's disappearance?

_____

_____

4. Why does the author state, "we may never know the whole story"? Use details from the passage to support your answer.

_____

_____

_____

_____

Reflect

Think about how the author presents the theories about Earhart's disappearance. How does it affect the readers' conclusions? Use evidence from the passage to support your answer.

_____

_____

_____

_____

_____

_____

_____

Name _____

Read the passages on pages 58 and 60. Then, answer the questions.

1. Both passages focus on Amelia Earhart's final flight around the world and her disappearance. Yet, they are very different in several ways. Explain how the passages are different.

_____

_____

_____

_____

2. What shocking fact does "Where Is Amelia?" mention that isn't mentioned in "A Challenge to Others"?

_____

3. How does this fact affect the reader's opinion about Earhart?

_____

_____

4. Compare and contrast the authors' opinions of Amelia in both passages.

_____

_____

_____

_____

☀ Reflect

How do the authors' different opinions affect the readers? Use evidence from each passage to support your answer.

_____

_____

_____

_____

_____

_____

Answer Key

Answers will vary but may include the answers provided. Accept all reasonable answers as long as students have proper evidence and support.

Page 5
1. Seth was known as "the laziest kid in the class." Kyle thought he would probably have to do all of the work. 2. He was surprised to find out how knowledgeable and prepared Seth was. 3. Kyle changed from disappointed to confident about working with Seth. Check students' evidence.

Page 6
1. He was too old to work and his master was going to "do away with him." 2. All of the animals are described as "old." 3. Animals cannot sing, and their sounds would not combine in a beautiful way. 4. It helped them startle and scare away the robbers.

Page 7
1. He is working hard at school. 2. His mom is upset and doesn't understand how he is using the supplies so quickly. 3. because he is giving supplies to a student who can't afford them

Page 9
1. time flew: time passed quickly; talk my ear off: talk a lot; pulling my leg: tricking me; hit the road: started traveling; shoot the breeze: chat, or talk about nothing important; 2. They fish, play checkers, play games, take walks, and tell stories. 3. times when Grandpa tells stories about his past; 4. The narrator really enjoys time spent with Grandpa, especially the "remembering" times.

Page 11
1. The door was locked, and he knew it was after his mom should have been home. 2. His throat tightened, and he almost started to cry. 3. His mom's boss said she had left work on time. 4. anxious and worried; His mom apologized and hugged Derrick. She said all she could think about was Derrick waiting for her.

Page 13
1. They are pointed at the top like arrows, and they are pointing to their destination. 2. The narrator really likes the hike. 3. *wonderful, brightly, beautiful,* and *I love this place!* 4. The whole family enjoys it. The parents are excited to share their love of hiking, the narrator is excited about new experiences, and Ben is unhappy about not being able to bring a friend.

Page 15
1. The marina didn't have any available docks. 2. The author states that Tia is scared and afraid. She was shaking due to fear and has worried thoughts. 3. They are silent before and after the storm. However, before the storm they are relaxed because they listen to music and have a meal. After the storm, they are serious.

Page 16
1. He wants to win fights. Students should underline, "'Because if I was bigger I could win fights,' the man replied…" 2. The owl's question makes the man consider if he needs what he is wishing for. 3. Do not bother wishing for things you do not need.

Page 18
1. Bluebird wished to be the same blue color as the lake. She swam in the lake four times every day for five days and sang a special song. 2. the water; 3. He wanted to "be blue and beautiful too!" 4. pride; He was too concerned about making sure everyone saw his new color, so he didn't look where he was going.

Page 19
1. "His wings were made of rainbow feathers, and his voice was the sweetest ever heard." 2. It burnt his tail feathers, turned him black, and destroyed his voice. 3. The Great Sky Spirit gives him the gift of freedom from being hunted by man. Man would not want his meat or plain feathers, but crow could still see the rainbow colors reflecting in the black.

Page 21
1. They had no children. 2. They create a snow child. 3. She knew she would disappear when spring arrived. Check students' reasoning. 4. Her song explains how she arrives in winter and leaves in spring. It

tells them that she will always return because she loves her parents. 5. in a very painful, sad way; They were extremely sad and believed that she was not coming back.

Page 22
1. whipping, 'round; 2. It wouldn't describe the roughness or the effect the curves had on the narrator as well. 3. *like a snake, coiling 'round and 'round, The whipping of the curves, swings me like a bell, whipping path*

Page 23
1. to deal with emotions, how to try again, and to love, laugh, live, work, share, and give; 2. You can succeed after failing if you try again. 3. so the author can reach his or her full potential and make someone proud

Page 24
1. The turtle's "room" is his shell, which is free. 2. to start traveling; Runner doesn't fly like the cuckoos do. 3. an elephant's snout; a large case used for transporting items while traveling; The author used both meanings to show the humor that an elephant travels with a trunk, but it is not the same trunk people travel with.

Page 25
1. The narrator sees the wind move kites, birds, and ladies' skirts; feels the wind push; and hears it rustle. 2. Students should circle the last two lines of each stanza. 3. The wind can be heard rustling, and makes itself "loudly" known in other ways.

Page 27
1. "How strange life would be!" 2. They are nice to think about but too strange to be a part of real life. 3. *good, wild,* and *free*; 4. They are exciting and open up a world of possibilities.

Page 28
1. Animals sleep in many different ways. 2. Each paragraph explains a different way animals may sleep and gives supporting examples. 3. Both animals and humans need to sleep. Humans sleep inside on a bed or mat each night and don't sleep in large groups. Most animals do not require something to sleep on or shelter to sleep under. Animals may sleep in groups and at different times of day.

Page 29
1. It looked like a duck mixed with a beaver. Features like short legs, webbed feet, extra fur, and spurs made it look even stranger. 2. baby platypuses; 3. It is a strange term that most people have not heard, so it can make a weird animal seem even weirder.

Page 30
1. Only female mosquitoes bite people. 2. Only females need the protein from blood to hatch healthy eggs. 3. the long, thin mouth of a mosquito; The proboscis is used to inject a chemical that causes an itchy allergic reaction and to remove blood.

Page 31
1. The males, not the females, carry the young. 2. their life cycle; 3. their scientific name means "horse sea monster," they use camouflage, they are small and can be a variety of colors and patterns, males take care of the young

Page 32
1. To honor Sue Hendrickson, who discovered the fossil. 2. It is the largest, most complete, and best preserved *T. rex* ever found. 3. Scientists can study a well-preserved and mostly complete skeleton to learn more about dinosaurs.

Page 34
1. an orphaned leopard cub; 2. Harriet was an orphan, so Billy Arjan Singh took her in and helped her learn how to survive in the wild. 3. He had trained her so she could live in the wild without human help. 4. She brought her cubs to stay at his farm. She also jumped in his boat and waited for Billy to see her and understand she wanted a ride across the river. 5. Usually humans and wild animals are not

connected. Harriet's trust was a connection between them, like a bridge.

Page 35

1. They are important vocabulary words. 2. cats; They are curious and will approach boats full of people. 3. during their migration; Because they stay in warm, shallow water near the coast, it is easier for people to travel to them.

Page 37

1. queen, soldier, worker; 2. Driver Ant Colonies; 3. Worker ants help feed soldiers, the colony makes a nest out of their own bodies for the queen and grubs, and they build a bridge or ball out of ants to cross or float across a stream. 4. by protecting the queen and workers; They must rely on the worker ants to feed them. 5. A colony of driver ants works together to survive. The sentence mentions how well they cooperate.

Page 38

1. punched with holes so it tears easily; 2. The company was not looking to create a disposable hand towel. The paper mill made a mistake with the type of tissue it sent. 3. No one created the material on purpose. They just found a way the mistake could be useful.

Page 39

1. the Mayans and others; 2. He added flavoring. 3. The author doesn't understand why Adams has been forgotten even though he created a very popular product that is still used today.

Page 40

1. It does not have any freshwater, and there is so much salt in it that plants and animals cannot live there. 2. The lake has no outlet, so as the water evaporates, the salt is left behind. 3. It is surrounded by land and fed by a river. It does not have freshwater, and no plants or animals live in it.

Page 41

1. It is one of the worst because every building was damaged or completely gone, and more than 6,000 people died. 2. The people rebuilt their city, including a tall, thick seawall to protect the city in the future. 3. Check students' underlining.

Page 42

1. He holds a world record for the most times a person has been struck by lightning. 2. He learned a lot about lightning and became a weather watcher. 3. While Sullivan holds a record for being struck the most times by lightning, it is a very dangerous thing.

Page 44

1. They believed a person would die if they traveled by balloon. 2. the length of the first hot air balloon flight with passengers; 3. If the animals had not flown safely in the air for some time, no one would have trusted hot air balloon travel for humans. Because they did it, hot air balloons have been improved over time and become very popular. 4. Ed Yost helped design and create hot air balloons. He worked with the navy and made important changes in their design.

Page 46

1. glowing and reddish-orange; The strange thing about them is that they move up and down, change speed, and disappear suddenly. 2. a thought or belief about a set of facts; 3. People think that they are headlights of cars, campfires of the Apaches, moonlight reflecting off of minerals, or gas from swamps. The Apaches think they are stars that have fallen to Earth. Scientists think the lights may be reflected light from planets or stars. 4. the Apache and scientists; The Apache thought the lights were stars that had fallen to Earth. Scientists think they may be starlight reflecting off of the hills.

Page 47

1. a low place between mountains; 2. The coldest air is held between the mountains, so the town stays colder than the surrounding areas. 3. The town of Verkhoyansk, Russia, is one of the coldest and harshest places to live in the northern hemisphere.

Page 48

1. velocipede, boneshaker; 2. It started without pedals, had a large front wheel, and was made of wood. Then, pedals were added and front tires were changed so that they could turn when steered. Finally, air-filled tires and brakes were added. 3. The invention of cars made bikes less popular for traveling.

Page 50

1. success and good fortune, especially with money; 2. He is excited. Yes, because many immigrants felt that going to America would change their lives in a good way. Check students' evidence. 3. Both passages mention that the men in the family move to America while the women stay in China and that some Chinese men have their own laundry businesses. The "Chinese Immigrants" passage states that some men were disappointed and didn't get as much money as they had hoped and that they had fewer rights than Americans. The journal entries describe the boat ride to the New World but don't mention if the father enjoys being in America. 4. Both terms imply a sense of hope about the opportunities available in America.

Page 51

1. his discoveries with electricity; 2. Franklin did many important things in his lifetime. 3. Each paragraph describes a different way he made a difference in the world. The paragraphs discuss his accomplishments as a printer, a statesman, and an inventor.

Page 53

1. a false name taken by a performer; The boy's name was Jean François Gravelet, but he later changed his name to Charles Blondin. 2. Both times he knew immediately that he had to do something. 3. a fantastic act of skill; He crossed Niagara Falls on a tightrope. He also stood on a chair, pushed a wheelbarrow, walked blindfolded, and cooked and ate some eggs while on a tightrope. 4. Charles Blondin was a performer famous for his tightrope feats. The illustration shows him on a tightrope in a fancy outfit made for performances.

Page 54

1. She was accepted into Juilliard at five years old, played in orchestras, and recorded CDs before she was 10. 2. She enjoys playing the violin and making music for other people to enjoy. She doesn't like having her entire life planned and not having free time. 3. the human voice; It tells you that she feels familiar with the violin and music.

Page 56

1. a female journalist who set a new world record for a trip around the world; 2. Women rarely traveled alone or over long distances. 3. First, Bly's boss agreed to send her. She left New York City, traveled to England and then to France, where she met Jules Verne. Next, she traveled to Egypt, Yemen, and Sri Lanka. Finally, she reached San Francisco and sped to New York City by train. 4. She introduced people to new cultures through her newspaper articles. She also proved that women could travel alone and go on adventures.

Page 57

1. Ty Cobb was the meanest player of all time. 2. He had a temper and attitude. He started fights and caused injuries. He may have played with sharpened spikes to hurt other players on purpose. 3. Though he was disliked by many people, Cobb was a talented baseball player.

Page 59

1. She was the first woman to fly across the Atlantic Ocean and the only person to do it twice. 2. She was successful in her flights, so she felt capable of trying to break a new record. She was also influenced by the successes of men, such as Charles Lindbergh. 3. It shows Earhart's attitude toward equal rights and failure. The passage describes her actions and how they were inspired by the successes of men.

Page 61

1. to quickly or mysteriously disappear; 2. It would make her disappearance seem less strange. 3. She ran out of gas and crashed into the ocean, or she had problems during a spying mission. 4. There is no proof of how or why she crashed, and her plane and body have never been recovered.

Page 62

1. The first passage discusses her background and past experiences. The second passage explains her final trip in more detail, mentions that she was suspected to be a spy, and includes facts about present day. 2. She was possibly a spy. 3. Readers may feel that Earhart had lied and tricked people. Or, they may think she was even braver and patriotic. 4. Both authors appreciate her successes. The author of the first passage has a positive opinion about Earhart and her accomplishments. The author of the second passage shares that Earhart is more mysterious than people first thought.